# TIME TO LEAVE

# JOHN IRVIN

**Other works by John Irvin:**

<u>Series:</u>

Tales of Time: Book 1, Extraordinary Lives

<u>Novels:</u>

Longevity

<u>Politics:</u>

Libertarianism vs Constitutionalism

Time To Leave

"The Union next to our liberties the most dear. May we all remember that it can only be preserved by respecting the rights of the States, and distributing equally the benefits and burdens of the Union."

John C. Calhoun

# Preface

Secession—such a mysterious and almost notorious word. Thanks to over a century of pro-Northern brainwashing, the majority of Americans are leery and contemptuous when this word is brought up. Immediately their minds pounce upon the Cause of the South during the alleged "American Civil War" that took place 150 years ago. They immediately think of the Yankee myth of racist bigots who sought to destroy our National government and tear our Country apart. But the question remains, why was the War fought? Why did Lincoln send hundreds of thousands of Americans to their deaths? Was it really over slavery?

In the past 20 years or so it seems the number of books, articles, and other works defending the Cause of the South has grown exponentially. Why is this do you suppose? I believe it is because truth conquers all. But under a government of lies truth becomes treason. But if this be treason, make the most of it.

The federal government has overreached its Constitutional boundaries. That should be very clear and plain to see. But many have chosen to finally take a stand and get involved. But their hope is to "restore the Constitutional boundaries" and "return the checks and balances" within and over this present national government. We commend them for this optimistic hope but according to the experiences of history we do not believe that will ever happen to America as a whole. Over two-hundred years ago our Founding Fathers hoped for the same reconciliation. They protested, they petitioned, they did everything in their power to restore the constitutional bounds on their government. They tried everything until they realized they only had one last resort—secession, they called it the Declaration of Independence.

Secession is by definition merely the going out from a compact—separation from the rule of one government and forming a new government. Its beginning is no longer recognizing the legitimacy of one government's rule and its end would be recognizing a new government's rule. This idea has very deep Biblical and historical roots.

Thousands of years ago, the people of Israel had moved to Egypt and placed themselves under the Egyptian government. They made a compact with this government for protection and provision while they swore obedience. Many years afterward the Egyptian government became unbearably cruel and oppressive. The Hebrews were enslaved. Then God sent along a deliverer—Moses. After petitioning the king and being refused, Moses led the people of Israel out from Egypt with God's help. This is the first Biblical account of a national secession.

Many hundreds of years later, after King Solomon had died and his son Rehoboam took the throne. The representatives of the people of Israel convened with him and asked him to lighten up the tax load and other laws. Rehoboam went to his advisors, both elder and younger. He listened to his peers and decided that he would bear down even harder—he would raise the taxes and increase regulations. The representatives of Israel, excluding those of the tribe of Judah, called out in 1 Kings 12:16, *"What portion have we in David? neither have we inheritance in the son of Jesse: to your tents, O Israel: now see to thine own house, David."*

They argued that they no longer had a say in their government therefore they decided to declare their independence. And they did.

A third Hebrew example of secession would be that of the Hebrews and their attempt to secede from the Roman Empire. This attempt was a failure and it ended with the Temple in Jerusalem being destroyed and many Jews being slaughtered by the Romans.

A fourth historical example would be that of the nation of Scotland in the early fourteenth century. Almost everyone in America and in Scotland today knows of the film *Braveheart* and its portrayal of the Scottish War for Independence. It is based on a true account. Sir William Wallace, the leader of the resistance (according to Edward Longshanks of England—the tyrant who was seeking to usurp the rule over Scotland—it was a rebellion), led his countrymen against the tyrannical rule of England. He was martyred in 1305 but Robert the Bruce took up the leadership of the Cause and led Scotland to victory in 1314.

Finally a more recent account would be that of the Soviet Union. Back in the late '80's and early '90's, the world watched as the "mighty" Soviet Union broke apart into many different nations. The many nations seceded from the Union successfully. The dictator, Gorbachev, after a long few years of attempting to "preserve the Union" finally conceded the power and allowed the people to leave and form their own governments to govern their own nations.

Now most freedom-loving Americans today would claim that they are happy for the people of Eastern Europe and many cheered on this massive secessionist movement of the 20th Century. Why are they so posed to support this while at the same time being opposed to a secessionist movement here in the United States of America? Say for example, the War for Southern Independence? How can they be opposed to that war while being staunch supporters of the American Revolution? It is astounding and heart-wrenching to see just how far we have been brainwashed by the pro-Yankee (pro-Central government) propaganda over the past century and a half.

This booklet's goal will be to convey the three American secession movements in their true similar lights. Two have already been fought—one was a success the other a failure. And one is yet to happen. It will be up to you to decide.

# The First Secession

"Caesar had his Brutus! Charles the First his Cromwell! And George the Third may profit from their example." Patrick Henry declared, his voice firm and courageous. The Chairman of the House of Burgesses in which Mr. Henry was presiding, cried out, "Treason!" Patrick Henry did not flinch as he finished his declaration calmly but unyielding. "If this be treason...make the most of it."

These were very dangerous words for a single man to say at this time. Emotions were high as the thought of possible outright rebellion by force of arms was on the mind of every man that day. The House of Burgesses was meeting in Virginia to discuss the tyrannical moves that their king had been making recently. The thought of taking up arms against their government was definitely treasonous to many of them and to some it was even an abomination against God.

Time after time the American Colonies sent petition after petition pleading with their government against its actions taken against their liberties. The majority of the Colonists believed that being English citizens they possessed every right and liberty passed down to them by their forefathers through the British constitution and laws. They believed in the doctrine of "social compact." A compact was made all the way back during the time of King John of England and his signing of the Magna Carta with the nobles of the land. This compact and the laws and constitution that followed were based on this and designed to protect the liberties of the people.

After the French and Indian War the English government noticed the growing economy of its American Colonies. Because the Colonists used mostly a free trade policy and Biblical/capitalistic ethics their revenue was steadily increasing. Their English government decided they would reap this escalating revenue. So Parliament began its infamous tax levying and assaults on the rights of the

Colonists. The people were treated as second-class citizens. Then came the Boston Massacre. The spark was lit. Next the Tea Parties were organized and protests spread across the Colonies. And finally, at Lexington, the spark broke into a wildfire at the sound of the first shot of the American Revolution.

John Dickinson penned what is known as the Olive Branch petition. This petition was an attempt to assert the rights of the Colonists while promising their continued allegiance to the British government. The Continental Congress adopted this petition on July 5, 1775. They sent it to King George in hopes that they could keep from all out civil war. The king refused to even read the petition and declared the American Colonies had "proceeded to open and avowed rebellion." According to him the Colonists were rebelling against his supreme authority. All authority must be obeyed, right?

I have discussed this issue more than I care to be honest. I believe the answer—according to the Holy Scriptures—that not all authority is to be obeyed. There is such a thing as illegitimate authority. Many scholars and philosophers have given countless treatises on this certain topic. John Locke would be one such philosopher. In his *Two Treatises on Government*, Locke sets forth an argument against the false doctrine of the "divine right of kings." (The belief that anything a ruler says or commands is of God and must be obeyed). Locke—using Scripture verses over 200 times in his Treatises on Government—declares that this is definitely not so.   Other scholars would include Sir William Blackstone and his *Commentaries on the Laws of England*. Another would be the not so well known—in the political realm—John Milton. Known for his most popular work *Paradise Lost*, Milton was actually a very prominent defender of the Revolution against Charles the First. His many political works include, *Areopagitica, The Tenure of King's and Magistrates*, *Defence of the People of England, Second Defence of the People of England,* and *The Readie and Easie Way to Establish a Free Commonwealth*. Milton is actually referred to as the "Father of Secession." Another individual would be Reverend Jonathan Mayhew. A contemporary of the First Great Awakening, Mayhew is credited for the first usage of the phrase "no taxation without representation." One of his most prominent works is a discourse he wrote by the name of *A Discourse Concerning Unlimited Submission and Non-Resistance to the Higher Powers*. It is within this work that the Reverend Mayhew presents a very thorough argument for resistance against tyranny and his whole foundation is built mostly on Romans 13. One more scholar I would mention who was also a minister as Mayhew is the Reverend Charles Chauncy. Both Chauncy and Mayhew were members of the "Black Regiment," an organized movement of ministers and clergy who opposed the tyrannical rule of their British government and taught from the Holy Word that at times resistance—whether non-violent or violent—was an inalienable right given by God Himself. These men argued for their countries—Locke, Milton, Blackstone in England and Mayhew and Chauncy in the American Colonies. These men and so many others stood for the right of the people to dissolve the political bands that had connected them to one government for so long and to assume among the powers of the earth a new government. This is the very principle stated in the very first paragraph of the birth certificate of these united States—the Declaration of Independence.

"When in the course of human events it becomes necessary for one people to *dissolve* the political bands which have connected them with another and to assume among the powers of the earth, the *separate* and *equal* station to which the Laws of Nature and of Nature's God entitle them..." (Italics added for emphasis)

These very lines describe to the tee what our Founding Fathers and the many scholars before them believed to be a God-given law of nature. That if any government became tyrannical and usurped powers outside of the Law—and that is ultimately Natural Law, laid down by the Creator—then the compact between them and the people that they had been given the responsibility to govern and protect was broken—dissolved, void.

Most people do not realize the true thought and substance of this blood-signed document. Yet it is very clearly written right there on that old artifact that our Founding Fathers were declaring their Secession from the British Empire. The very first paragraph says it so clearly the only way they could have been clearer would to have simply said, "We are seceding from Great Britain." How clear is this? "To dissolve the political bands which have connected them with another, and to assume among the powers of the earth the separate and equal station..." Separate? Dissolve the political bands and become independent by separating themselves from the old government. Separation is Secession. Secession is Separation. And what did they say about this separation? "The laws of nature and of nature's God entitle them." Secession is a Natural Right endowed by the Creator Himself.

Now many believe that this Declaration was the birth certificate for a new Nation. I believed this for a long time as well. Now I do believe it was the birth certificate of these united States. But it did not establish any form of government, did not set up any governing body, did not create any laws or regulations, therefore, it did not form a nation. The Declaration of Independence did nothing but just that, it declared our intent to secede and become independent. The Articles of Confederation followed by the Constitution were the documents that established an actual governing body. Even the words of the Declaration state it very clearly in the last paragraph. "...in the name and by the authority of the good people of these Colonies, solemnly publish and declare that *these* United Colonies are, and of right ought to be, *free* and *independent* States...and that as *free* and *independent States*, they have full power to levy war, conclude peace, contract alliance, establish commerce, and do all other acts and things which *independent States* may of right do." (Italics used for emphasis) Notice the emphasis that our Fathers placed on the words Free and Independent States. A state in itself is its own nation--for what is a nation but a people and their chosen government. These States recognized though that they were united in a common cause and that was to throw off the tyrannical chains of the government. But nowhere did they ever declare that this union could never be dissolved--I think it odd as would anyone else with common sense think it if they had at the same time declared that no one could dissolve that compact seeing as they had just dissolved the one with their British government.

And dissolve it they did. And by the grace of God they fought and won their freedom and independence. Many years later, after finally convincing the people that the Articles of Confederation did not work, the Constitutional Convention was convened and an arduous struggle to form a new government was fought. They were attempting to form a government that would be strong enough to protect the people and keep order between the states while at the same time be too weak to attack that most precious gift given to us by our Creator--besides salvation--our Liberty. An interesting note about the Articles of Confederation, which declared a "perpetual Union", it also proclaims Article II that, "Each State retains its sovereignty, freedom, and independence, and every power, jurisdiction, and right, which is not by this Confederation expressly delegated to the United States, in Congress assembled." The thing about "delegated" powers or abilities, they can be reclaimed. An entity or party may delegate to another party certain authorities but that first party is still the delegator, merely using the second party as an agent to perform the duties the first party wishes it to do. If the party that has been given those powers does something the delegator does not approve of the delegator may reclaim those delegated powers whenever it wishes. When the Founding Fathers said, "a perpetual Union", they were merely wishing that the States would always live in harmony with each other. But nowhere in the United States Constitution can those words or anything similar to them be found. Obviously someone recognized that sometimes contracts are broken, dissolved, or simply expire. There were those who stood against forming a new governing document. They believed the Articles of Confederation would be the better form if it were only modified. Even the great Orator of the American Revolution, Patrick Henry, declared, "I smell a rat." He led the party known as the Anti-Federalists. But what was it that he and so many like him did not trust about this new Constitution? Centralizing of power into a national government is the answer. This step took power from the States and gave it to the central government; this was an attack against one of the checks and balances they had laid down. While the others—the Federalists—believed that it would be in the United States best interest to consolidate more power into the central government. George Mason, a member of the Anti-Federalist party, gave a warning against the Constitution at the Virginia Ratification Convention when Virginia was deciding whether to join the new Union that had been set up under the Constitution. George Mason warned,

> Whether the Constitution be good or bad, the present clause clearly discovers, that it is a National Government, and no longer a confederation. I mean that clause which gives the first hint of the General Government laying direct taxes. The assumption of this power of laying direct taxes, does of itself, entirely change the confederation of the States into one consolidated Government. This power being at discretion, unconfined, and without any kind of controul, must carry every thing before it. The very idea of converting what was formerly a confederation, to a consolidated Government, is totally subversive of every principle which has hitherto governed us. This power is calculated to annihilate totally the State Governments. Will the people of this great community submit to be individually taxed

by two different and distinct powers? Will they suffer themselves to be doubly harrassed? These two concurrent powers cannot exist long together; the one will destroy the other: The General Government being paramount to, and in every respect more powerful than, the State governments, the latter must give way to the former. Is it to be supposed that one National Government will suit so extensive a country, embracing so many climates, and containing inhabitants so very different in manners, habits, and customs? It is ascertained by history, that there never was a Government, over a very extensive country, without destroying the liberties of the people: History also, supported by the opinions of the best writers, shew us, that monarchy may suit a large territory, and despotic Governments over so extensive a country; but that popular Governments can only exist in small territories. Is there a single example, on the face of the earth, to support a contrary opinion? Where is there one exception to this general rule? Was there ever an instance of a general National Government extending over so extensive a country, abounding in such a variety of climates, &c. where the people retained their liberty? I solemnly declare, that no man is a greater friend to a firm Union of the American States than I am: But, Sir, if this great end can be obtained without hazarding the rights of the people, why should we recur to such dangerous principles?[1]

Well, was he right? Yes, the Constitution worked for a while. It seemed to be the best form of government ever laid down by man in the history of the world. Yet even still—with an almost perfect document—false and designing

[1] Storing, Herbert J., ed. *The Complete Anti-Federalist.* 7 vols. Chicago: University of Chicago Press, 1981.

men were able to creep their way in and find means to subvert and twist such a wonderful document.

# The Second Secession

Almost everyone knows the Gettysburg Address, given by Abraham Lincoln on November 19, 1863 at Gettysburg just after a very bitter victory had been won there by the Union. Everyone knows that famous line, "That government of the people, by the people, for the people, shall not perish from the earth," or the opening words, "Four score and seven years ago our fathers brought forth upon this continent, a new nation..."

But what most do not know is the inaccuracies and outright lies that fill this speech—the hypocrisy and total anti-American actions of this world-renown President of the United States.

Let us start with the opening lines of Lincoln's famous speech. He declared, "Four score and seven years ago our fathers brought forth upon this continent, a new nation, conceived in Liberty, and dedicated to the proposition that all men are created equal." According to Lincoln, the American nation was "brought forth" 87 years before 1863. That would mean that the United States was formed in the year 1776. So in his eyes, the Declaration of Independence formed the United States. Now as I have mentioned before, the Declaration of Independence was not a government document—it did not set up any institution or form of government. In Lincoln's eyes the national government had been formed when our Founding Fathers had signed that document. Tell me, where in the Declaration of Independence is there any hint of a laying down of governing rules, or setting up of any political office of any sort whatsoever? There is none.

And the final lines of Lincoln's Gettysburg Address speaks of the consent of the governed, "That we here highly resolve that these dead shall not have died in vain -- that this nation, under God, shall have a new birth of freedom – and that government of the people, by the people, for the people, shall not perish from the earth."

The Union's victory was surely a new birth of something—not freedom. And Mr. Lincoln ended his beloved speech declaring that government by the consent of the governed would not perish from the earth as if the South had wished to destroy that. As if the South had invaded and was attempting to destroy everything our Founding Fathers had pledged their lives for.

But seeing as legitimate government is founded upon the consent of the governed, should not the people have a say on how they are ruled? Should they not have the right to be represented? And if a people's voice—whether a majority or a minority—has no hope of ever being represented by their government, should they not have the unalienable right to "dissolve the political bands" that have connected them to that government and to "assume among the powers of the earth that separate and equal station to which the Laws of Nature and of Nature's God entitle them"? Is that not the American idea?

Sadly most people do not know the hypocrisy of Lincoln. Even he recognized the right of the people to secede from their government and form a new government. Lincoln declared in a speech in the United States House of Representatives on January 12, 1848, "Any people anywhere being inclined and having the power have the right to rise up and shake off the existing government, and form a new one that suits them better. This is a most valuable, a most sacred right — a right which we hope and believe is to liberate the world. Nor is this right confined to cases in which the whole people of an existing government may choose to exercise it. Any portion of such people that can may revolutionize and make their own of so much of the territory as they inhabit."

In his own words, the man contradicted his own future actions.

So according to this it was Lincoln and his followers who destroyed the consent of the governed—it was they who caused that nation of the people, by the people, and for the people to perish from the earth.

Now the question of slavery. The "scholars" of pro-Lincoln Yankeedom always love to bring this issue up whenever the discussion of the War for Southern Independence is brought to the table. They always bring it up because it is their only apparent tool to be used to justify the illegal invasion of a free nation. And yet if one is wise he will seek after knowledge so that he may understand what happened and know the truth. The Lincoln-worshippers who have flooded the schools and libraries with their propaganda always declare that it was for the freeing of the slaves that Lincoln invaded the South.

Now the whole intent of this booklet is to argue for the case of secession so the focus will not be on slavery here. But I will give a few words on it. If you want to learn more, then I highly encourage you to read the amazing and fact-filled book, *The South Was Right!* by James Ronald Kennedy.

First off we will start with Lincoln's First Inaugural Address. He very clearly promised, "I have no purpose, directly or indirectly, to interfere with the institution of slavery in the States where it exists. I believe I have no lawful right to do so, and I have no inclination to do so."

So either "honest" Abe's war was merely to subject a free people into submission to the all-powerful federal government or he lied and his war was actually fought to free the slaves. Doesn't sound very honest to me.

"The Great Emancipator" is one who believed in the equality of the races and was willing to wage the bloodiest war in history at that time to free some, or so that's what the Lincoln idolaters tell us. Lincoln himself did not believe the two races would ever be equal. He was in fact a leader in the movement to recolonize the free blacks to the colony of Liberia or to their own native land. Being a leader in the newly formed Republican Party, Lincoln also either directly or indirectly worked on getting a Constitutional Amendment passed that would ban the federal government from ever dealing in the affairs of the institution of slavery.

If you would like to read more about Lincoln's views and actions toward racial issues I recommend Thomas DiLorenzo's great works, *The Real Lincoln* and *Lincoln Unmasked*.

The majority of the Northern states held the black-skinned people from the Dark Continent in contempt and disgust. In fact, according to true historical account and eye-witnesses, the slaves in the South lived in better conditions than the free blacks in the North. The French author, Alexis de Toqueville, who is well known for his work *Democracy in America*, has been referenced by many to describe society in America during his great tour of these States. In his work, he described the racial views of both sections of the nation.

> Whoever has inhabited the United States must have perceived that in those parts of the Union in which the Negroes are no longer slaves they have in no wise drawn nearer to the whites. On the contrary, the prejudice of race appears to be stronger in the states that have abolished slavery than in those where it still exists; and nowhere is it so intolerant as in those states where servitude has never been known.

So if freeing the slaves was not the true purpose behind invading the South, what was? Let us ask Lincoln himself for a very clear cut answer. When asked in Congress in 1846 why he would not let the South go peacefully, this "great Liberator" replied, "I can't let them go. Who would pay for the government?"

I can't go into great detail in this booklet on the financial support that the South was giving the federal government because of its free trade economy and low tariffs. The North, being industrial, was more progressive in its economy. And with the term "progressive" I am speaking of the economic view that eventually progresses into outright socialism. And in fact it was Lincoln who enacted the first income tax during the War. According to the *Communist Manifesto*, the income tax is the first step toward a socialist utopia. Because of the flourishing economy of the South, these states were the ones paying for most of the support of the federal government. A federal government that was becoming less and less federal. The Southern states were being forced to give more money than their Northern brethren to fund actions they did not approve of—such as nationalizing the railroad, involving the federal government more and more in internal affairs, higher tariff rates (i.e. the Tariff of Abominations), etc.

It was Thomas Jefferson—one of the most ardent patriots and a Southerner himself—who declared, "To compel a man to furnish funds for the propagation of ideas he disbelieves and abhors is sinful and tyrannical."

And this was the true reason why Lincoln invaded the South—because he wanted their money. If you would like to study more on the economic reasons for the war then a very good work would be Charles Adam's *When in the Course of Human Events*. This work presents a very detailed and the most unbiased case for the true reason the South was conquered.

Mr. Adam's even discusses the outside view on the War by several foreign nations such as Britain and France. Britain could not understand why Lincoln would wage war on those who wished for independence when only about 80 years prior the Americans had wished to declare their independence from Britain.

But no it was the Lincoln administration's lust for empire that drove him into this self-contradicting cultural genocide.

Another frighteningly disturbing fact is the birth of the Republican Party. Most today would consider the Republican Party the conservative party that has been attempting to hold the "socialistic" Democratic Party on the left from destroying the nation. But if one simply turns on the television to the news channel, it is very obvious that today neither side—right or left, conservative or liberal—stands for the Founding Principles written down in the Declaration of Independence itself. Both parties are on the same train—the GOP is simply a car or two behind—headed for the same cliff that will send us careening into the chasm of sure destruction. Most do not know about the birth of the Republican party. They do not know that this party was actually organized by Marxists, socialists, and imperialists. It was this party that was for nationalizing the railroad, increasing taxes, and building a world empire. In his book, *Lincoln Uber Alles*, John Avery Emison relates to us, through deep research, the influence that Karl Marx brought to our own home shores.

It was during the year of 1848 that Europe was boiling with revolution. Only it wasn't revolution like the Revolution that birthed America into being. These revolutions were organized and led by Marxists, including Karl Marx's own brother-in-law. These men were known as the Forty-Eighters. But things did not go well for these revolutionaries and many of them were forced to flee their native lands and escape to America. For lack of space, I cannot go into the detail I wish to delve into on this issue but you may and—if I may say—you must research this for yourself. I will bring up a couple facts though. Many of Lincoln's personal appointees, secretaries, and leading Union generals were either Forty-Eighters or their followers. A second fact—and the last one I will mention with this topic but I believe a very important one—is the origin of the Pledge of Allegiance.

Many call someone patriotic if they wish to recite the Pledge of Allegiance in schools or at games or rallies or wherever. But most do not know that the Pledge of Allegiance was part of the Republican agenda during the late 1800's to instill in the hearts and minds of the succeeding generations the worship of the

State—the American Empire. This pledge of "allegiance" would better be called a Pledge of "Worship of the Government."

The Pledge was written in August of 1892 by the socialist minister Francis Bellamy. He originally published it in *The Youth's Companion* on September 8, 1892. It originally read, "I pledge allegiance to my Flag and the Republic for which it stands, one nation, indivisible, with liberty and justice for all." The article in the *Companion* read,

> At a signal from the Principal the pupils, in ordered ranks, hands to the side, face the Flag. Another signal is given; every pupil gives the flag the military salute — right hand lifted, palm downward, to a line with the forehead and close to it. Standing thus, all repeat together, slowly, "I pledge allegiance to my Flag and the Republic for which it stands; one Nation indivisible, with Liberty and Justice for all." At the words, "to my Flag," the right hand is extended gracefully, palm upward, toward the Flag, and remains in this gesture till the end of the

affirmation; whereupon all hands immediately drop to the side.

*The Youth's Companion*, 1892

Shortly thereafter the salute was changed to starting with the right hand over the heart and after reciting "the Flag" the right arm was stretched outward, palm down, toward the Flag. But during World War II, this resembled too much the Nazi salute and it was changed to simply keeping the right hand over the heart.

It was not till 1954 that President Eisenhower, with the influence of the Roman Catholic Knights of Columbus, encouraged Congress to add the words—that supposedly Christianized it—"under God" to this recitation. Interesting fact, Bellamy's daughter was highly opposed to this alteration.

Now I will always respect Old Glory only in remembrance of what she once stood for and I will never recite the Pledge of Allegiance to the United States (which is the name of the central government) but give my own Pledge to the cause of Liberty and the Author of Liberty.

It is interesting when I am discussing the unconstitutional actions of Abraham Lincoln with someone—even a Southerner—they remark that they understand it but they believe he was still a good man—he had to be. But I'm not sure these people—many who I love as friends—understand the extent of the damage caused by that tyrant of the North. If one researches the actions taken by this man and the atrocities he is either directly or indirectly responsible for I do not believe one could agree that Lincoln was a "good man."

Again I wish I could give good detail on all the acts of this tyrant who became god. But there are already plenty of works out on this subject and the object of this booklet is not to discuss Lincoln, it is to present a discussion for secession. But I will give some examples just to wet your appetite and possibly move you to read the other works on Lincoln that I have already mentioned.

Did you know that Lincoln is directly responsible for the largest mass execution? He himself signed the order to slaughter a huge number of leaders of the Plains Indians. He was responsible for the mass genocide of these tribes. How could one be seeking to "free" a race in one section of the country while at the same time be seeking the absolute annihilation of another race in another region?

Another dictatorial act that this worshipped president did was sign the arrest warrant for a dissenting Supreme Court Chief Justice. An elderly man, Roger B. Taney, openly opposed Lincoln's call for volunteers to invade the Southern nation and his other tyrannical acts. Lincoln, in all the wrath of a dictator, issued an arrest warrant for the old man. Although this warrant was never served, the fact that the benevolent leader of the nation, who preached liberty and equality for all, would commit such a heinous act—a common action taken by any average dictator against those who oppose him—is disgusting. What happened to the right of free speech, written in the Constitution?

Lincoln was also responsible for the arrest and imprisonment of most of the state legislators of Maryland upon invading the state that had openly expressed support for the Southern cause. He was also responsible for shutting down newspapers and arresting their chiefs, who expressed opposition against the bloodlust of the Lincoln administration all across the Northern states. These are all major attacks on free speech which is protected by the Constitution which he, as President, swore, with his right hand on the Holy Bible, before God and all Americans, that he would uphold and defend.

Another vicious attack is the suspending of the right of *habeas corpus* and trial by civil courts. This in essence was a declaration of martial law—a power not given to the executive branch in the Constitution. According to the United States Constitution—the Supreme Law of the Land (and we were founded as a union under the Rule of Law not the Whims of Man)—it is the Congress that is given this authority—to suspend habeas corpus. This is a major usurpation against the freedoms given to us by the Founding Fathers. And along with this was the use of military tribunals to try citizens who have the right to be tried by civil courts and a jury of impartial peers. Being tried by a military tribunal that has declared you the enemy is definitely not a civil or impartial trial.

Finally the whole idea of raising an army and invading a State—which he argued was still a part of his so-called union—in order to coerce them back under his rule is, I believe, the final straw to break the camel's back—as it was for Kentucky, Arkansas, Maryland, Missouri, the Arizona Territory, the Cherokee nation (i.e. Oklahoma Territory) and others. Nowhere in the Constitution does it give the President the authority to invade a state by use of force. This is not the action of a president it is the action of a conqueror seeking to subject a people under his own rule. Not to mention the fact that he vowed in his First Inaugural address that he would never invade a state. He declared that he "denounce(s) the lawless invasion by armed force of the soil of any State or Territory, *no matter what pretext*, as among the gravest of crimes." (Italics added for emphasis)

These and many other illegal actions were perpetuated by the man who declared that he wished for "malice toward none." How can someone be responsible for so many heinous crimes and be a good person?

Now comes an interesting topic that most patriotic Americans for the most part do not think about—the illegality and devastation of the Reconstruction Era. It was during this period that an entire culture was nearly wiped completely out.

After their defeat, the Southern states were placed under military occupation for several years. They were not given true representation in Congress for quite some time. The interesting thing to note is that the Southern states had to be "readmitted" into the Union. But according to the administration that had just previously fought an entire war, no state could leave the indivisible Union. How can one be readmitted if they never left?

But an interesting thing to note is the fact that the Northern representatives voted to not allow the Southern states representation in the federal government. With this the federal government had a window of opportunity to pass several amendments to the United States Constitution. This is illegal and criminal and the act of a conqueror. If you would like to research more on the illegality of the Reconstruction so-called 13th Amendment then I highly suggest the *Demon of Discord* by Richard C. Green. The 14th Amendment as well was not ratified according the Constitutional procedures. David Lawrence is a scholar when it comes to the illegality of the

14th Amendment. And the 15th Amendment is also a very un-American amendment. *The South Was Right!* by James Ronald Kennedy and Walter Donald Kennedy has a very thought-provoking section devoted to this certain amendment and the problems it has caused us. People have been brainwashed to believe it is a truly-American amendment because it gives us the "right and freedom" to vote no matter what station we hold in life or what color our skin is or what our views are. This is actually a very subtle but destructive law. In the beginning you were not allowed to vote unless you owned property or a job—depending on which state. Think of the impact such a law would have if all the sluggards who refuse to work and live off of government welfare—mostly spending it on booze and drugs while they rape women and abuse children—were not allowed to vote. Their only motivation for selecting a candidate is which one will give them more government welfare. According to one of the first Americans and a Southerner himself, John Smith—who actually based his law off of Biblical principles— if ye shall not work neither shall ye eat. Think of the boost in our economy if the government would stop spending on welfare—which is not a power given them by the Constitution in the first place—and those people actually realized they had to work to make a living. I think this would actually turn out to be a big solver of our job problem and our government spending problem.

Then even though it is not a Reconstruction amendment, the 16th Amendment is also something to take note on. It was also not ratified by the correct number of States as required in the Constitution. Bill Benson is the best when it comes to tearing apart the lies that surround this hideous, socialist, and anti-American pseudo-law that the federal government and the bureaucracy has used to steal from us what is rightfully—by God's Law—ours. He has several works written and you can find them on his website, www.thelawthatneverwas.com. It was actually Lincoln who enacted the first income tax law during the War for Southern Independence; Karl Marx, the one who wrote a letter praising Lincoln, wrote an outline of the basic steps to create a socialist utopia—the first step was, instituting an income tax. Think of the impact having no income tax (and no IRS because of that) would have.

After seeing all the devastation caused to his country during the Reconstruction era, Robert E. Lee declared to a fellow loyal Southerner, Governor Fletcher Stockdale, "Governor, if I had foreseen the use those people designed to make of their victory, there would have been no surrender at Appomattox Courthouse; no sir, not by me. Had I foreseen these results of subjugation, I would have preferred to die at Appomattox with my brave men, my sword in my right hand."

If only he had refused to surrender perhaps, yes, they would have died or perhaps God would have performed a miracle and the victory could have been ours. But we must not linger in the past, we must learn from it so that we can use it for the present for the sake of a better future. It was President Jefferson Davis who promised in 1881 in address to the Mississippi legislature, "The principle for which we contend is bound to reassert its self, though it may be at another time and in another form...the contest is not over, the strife is not ended. It has only entered upon a new and enlarged arena."

Just because a nation is conquered it neither makes the conqueror the rightful or legal ruler nor does it eliminate the right of that nation to one day seek independence once again.

# The Third Secession

Now that we have established that secession is the sovereign right of any state, or people, it is time that we bring our focus from the past to the present. The issue of secession has seen an immense rise in discussion and growth with organizations and groups beginning to push for it more and more. These people recognize that the American Empire is on the very precipice of destruction—the world as we know it is near the end.

But unlike many who are pessimistic in their views of our Nation and freedom, there are those of us who believe there is a way to possibly return to the Nation we once were, based on Judeo-Christian principles of truth, justice, and freedom. And this return could possibly be obtained by way of secession.

Now many will cry that this call to secession would be the death of us, many would say no one who had any brains would be dumb enough to go for something so extreme. Some will say the States wouldn't want to leave the Union because it would hurt our economy, because of our security, or because that would give the liberals the edge in Congress.

In all honesty, yes, it will be an up-hill struggle. That is only because of how far we've let ourselves fall. But God promises through any struggle He will make a way. Is it about the money? Is it about this false-security we have allowed to hypnotize us into our complacent slumber? Or is it about freedom and passing that Torch of Liberty down to the next generation?

If we are unwilling to take the chance and possibly make ourselves able to pass down a new nation, based on the original Republic, founded on the Principles our Founding Fathers fought and died for then we are the most selfish, cowardly, and foolish people that walked the face of this world.

The call for independence has already been made by countless voices. The object of this booklet has been to discuss the right of Independence and now it is time to discuss the benefits of secession. If we may peaceably secede, this transition could be very easy and simple compared to the more possible way we will have to secede. I pray to God we may leave Washington, D.C. without having to shed any needless blood but history and reason reveal otherwise. But even if it does come down to an armed conflict we must not give up hope and we must make sure that we rely completely on our Creator for His guidance and power as did George Washington when he stood against the British oppressors.

And now we will discuss a few of the benefits of Independence if we decide that freedom is better than this slavery we call security.

## Cultural Independence

There are many different cultures within the borders of the American empire and a few are at war with each other. The multiculturistic indoctrination of the regime's education system has already birthed a generation that for the most part no longer sees itself as a citizenry of a sovereign nation but citizens of a global order. Nationalists are called bigots and out-of-date idiots.

Independence from the Empire will give us back the freedom to preserve our own separate cultural foundation. As a Southerner, I recognize the South has maintained its own culture since its birth over 400 years ago, a culture different and separate from that of the North and now the Pacific.

Independence would give us the ability to return to our Southern cultural heritage which was founded upon the Judeo-Christian religion and its Biblical principles. The other states, Western, Northern, or Pacific may preserve their own separate cultures also as their own separate federations.

The inherent and natural rights of man will be revered once again and protected against those who wish to usurp or violate them. Such rights as the right to life will be defended again; abortion will be recognized as what it truly is--murder--and will be dealt with as such. The rights of property and the pursuit of happiness will be protected against foreign and especially domestic attacks.

When a culture is founded on the Judeo-Christian principles then the highest institution--marriage--will be defended and protected as the mutual contract between one man and one woman under God. All other perversions of this holy institution will be recognized as not only an abomination to the people and their Creator but as treason against the nation and its government and will be dealt with as such.

Religion will once again be recognized as the right of the people, especially those of the Christian faith. The right to worship God in one's own way will not be discriminated, denounced, or discouraged by any governmental servant or institution. Prayer and the Holy Bible will be returned to the schools and government buildings as a recognition of not only the principles they stand for but the heritage that we were founded upon for which the Founding Fathers fought and died for. Any citizen will have the right and freedom to worship, whether alone or with others, wherever, whenever, and however he pleases, so long as it does not physically harm any person--if it is a Christian worship then there is no way that could happen.

And recognizing that we are separate people with our own individual cultures we will institute laws, bans, and counter-measures against such internationalist organizations as the United Nations, North American Trades Union, North American Union, and other such New World Order treaties and unions. As sovereign republics we will stand against the religion of the Devil called globalism.

## Economic Independence

As a Southerner I am seeking the independence of my own people. Given the freedom to form their own confederation once again, I believe the Southern nation (today that would be the original 13 Confederate States plus Oklahoma, Missouri, and Maryland) could become a very economically stable and successful country. I am for other states outside of the South forming confederations of their own and will seek friendly relations with them if possible.

Our Southern republican confederation would be able to abolish and eradicate all of the socialistic, Marxist, and anti-capitalistic taxes and economic "reforms." Such taxes would include: the social security tax, the income tax, the property tax, etc. Such taxes and other welfare subsidiaries or pensions are unholy and un-Biblical, not to mention un-American in the true sense of the name. I, for one, would like to see the only taxing ability for the new federal government to be that of enacting a Fair Tax; the states may seek other means for collecting revenue so long as they are not those means just mentioned above.

A major part about our economic independence and success would be a return to having a currency that is actually worth something and none of this printing as many reserve notes as we wish. We would see a return to the mandatory standard of having a gold-and-silver-bullion-backed currency.

As for government-ran welfare, there would be no such thing. Biblically and constitutionally the present federal government has no authority or right for the maintenance, preservation, or existence of the welfare state it has enslaved every one of us to. In the new republican confederation the federal as well as state governments would not be allowed to have anything to do with welfare. Common sense would allow, so I believe, locally-ran welfare although it will be highly encouraged that private or church organized welfare is the best state.

## Educational Independence

A simple return to a well-working education system could be obtained by simply following a few steps such as these listed below:

- Abolish the public school system

- Localize schools—no federal (national) or state unions or boards—set up local boards over local schools consisting of local parents
- Allow churches to run and oversee these schools
- Put the Bible and prayer back into the schools

As an independent republic we would be able to do just this and after such actions have gone into effect any governmental intervention of any sort whether federal or state will be banned and our people will be given full and rightful responsibility of the education of their children.

## Political Independence

Once we have declared our independence we would have the liberty to form new constitutional confederations of sovereign and independent States who separately maintain and control their internal affairs while working together with their sister States to conduct foreign affairs.

A needed step as well to recognize and establish States' rights once again is the return of the election of Senators back to the States. This would return State-representation back to the Senate while the people as a population are already represented in the House of Representatives. It would also bring back part of the lost balance between the federal and state governments.

When it comes to term limits I am a completely loyal advocate for such measures. One of the first steps in establishing the new republic will be to place term limits on both the Executive and Legislative branches of government--I am quite fond of the presidential term limit as established in the Constitution of the Confederate States of America which only allows one six-year term. As for the Judicial branch I would be for a total abolishment of the branch on the federal level and leave that to the States individually but if there needs to be a federal judicial branch I would advocate either term limiting or giving a clearer explanation for "bad behavior."

When it comes to the right to vote, that this right should only be given to citizens of the same country is a given. So this right will be given to any citizen of any State that is a member of the confederation. However, after studying history, I have come to the conclusion that it is very possible that taking away the requirement for voters to own property was a mistake. Whether I would be an advocate for a return to such requirement time will tell. Benjamin Franklin saw the ownership of land as a sign of citizenship; he wrote to William Straham in 1784 saying, "Every Man who comes among us, and takes up a piece of Land, becomes a Citizen, and by our Constitution has a Voice in Elections, and a share in the Government of the Country." It does make sense that those who own property would be more likely to be more responsible with their vote and actually care about the policies of those they vote for. Maybe a compromise would be to go for the in-between which would only require a citizen to hold a steady job in order to vote. This will all be up for discussion once the conventions begin.

## Secure Independence

Gouverneur Morris announced, "Americans need never fear their government because of the advantage of being armed, which the Americans possess over the people of almost every other nation."

The right to own, carry, and use weapons for defense is the most sacred right for without it we are unable to defend all the others. We could speak against a tyrant but all he would have to do is arrest or execute us. It is our freedom to "keep and bear arms" that protects our liberty.

Recognizing this Biblically fundamental truth our republican confederation would recognize the true meaning and importance of the Second Amendment to the United States Constitution--although, I would prefer we maintain a separate Article in the Constitution for the "Bill of Rights" instead of declaring them through amendments. And the true meaning of the Second Amendment would be that every legal citizen of any of the individual, sovereign member states of the confederation would hold the recognized and irrevocable right to own, keep, and carry any firearm--or weapon used for defense for that matter--without any government interference in any form, such as permits, licenses, and other such infringing "requirements."

As we do believe in defending our international borders as well, we would agree there should be some form of military structure. But recognizing, as did Patrick Henry, Jefferson, and other Anti-Federalists, standing armies have been the most common tools of dictators in subduing the people. They say it is for our safety--that is when we should most fear them. Therefore, we would like to see a return to State militias and the abolishment of standing armies as the American federation relied on during the early years under the U.S. Constitution. And as was commonly known back then a militia consisted of every able-bodied citizen with a gun. This would be closely similar to the Swiss-style military.

Perhaps a State-regulated requirement for all 18 year-old male citizens of a 2 year program of training would produce a more vigilant defense. This would be only a decision given to the individual States with the Federal government having no say in the matter. And at the end of his training program each citizen would be awarded a firearm of his choice along with a regulated amount of ammunition. Now this would by no means take away any citizen's freedom to buy, sell, or own other weapons but would at least set a standard of at least one firearm for every household. What foreign nation would be stupid enough to attack such a well-armed population?

The borders will definitely be a top priority along with immigration and we hold that the strictest measures will be enacted. Both the federal government as well as the State to which an immigrant may wish to reside in will have a hand in the processing, while the individual State holds the regulative authority over the granting of citizenship.

And as a whole, the new republican confederation will hold a strict foreign policy of vigilant neutrality. It is to the wise and foreseeing words of two of the greatest presidents ever to serve under the U.S. Constitution, George Washington and Thomas Jefferson, that we will hold commerce and friendship with all, entangling alliances with none. We are not seeking any superiority or predominance over any other nation, we do not wish to be the bully who coerces other peoples into "following our example" whether we believe our example is right or not; all we wish is to be granted our rightful place among the nations of the earth and all we ask is to be left alone.

Already the recognition of the necessity of independence if we wish to be free has been steadily growing. Organizations and institutions have been springing up all over these united States seeking independence. Even some major TV/radio talk show hosts have begun to discuss the growing necessity and its benefits. The strongest supporters I would say are still here in the South with such organizations as the League of the South, the Southern Nationalist Network, the Southern National Congress, the Confederate Society of America, the Sons of Confederate Veterans, etc. And we all are seeking one goal--a sovereign and independent nation of our own, a new Confederation founded upon the Fundamental Principles for which the Founding Fathers and our Southern forefathers fought, bled, and died for. But the right and duty of independence is not just for the Southern states but for any state who wishes to free itself from the chains of this despotic regime that has--I believe--already destroyed the true America in the whole sense of the word. I believe, in order for Liberty to survive, it is necessary that the Empire be broken. I would love to see the American Empire broken up into maybe five or seven new republics based on truth, justice, freedom, and self-government. Let us remember, Liberty foremost before our Union. Which do we love more? Liberty or this Empire which we call a Union? (A true Union as everyone should already recognize is a mutual and voluntary contract between two or more parties, the present United States is not a true Union but an Empire with, at the present, fifty subjugated provinces) If you love Liberty then with all our heart we ask you, join us!

Time will tell if you are too late.